For the children of America
who hold the future of coins in their hands.

A SPECIAL MESSAGE

At Whitman Brands™, we believe that every coin tells a story, and there's no better way to spark curiosity and adventure than through collecting! *Kids Love Coins!* is designed to inspire young collectors, helping them discover the fun, history, and excitement behind a hobby that we're truly passionate about. Whether you're just starting your collection or adding to a growing one, we hope this book fuels a lifelong passion for numismatics. Let's pass on the love of collecting to future generations—one coin at a time!

Kids Love Coins!

4001 Helton Dr., Florence, AL 35630
whitman.com

Correspondence concerning this book may be directed to the publisher,
Attn: *Kids Love Coins!*, at the address above.

ISBN: 978-07948-53952 / ZT 1848 05/25
Printed in China.

ABOUT THE AUTHOR

Charles Ghigna - Father Goose® is a poet, children's author, and nationally syndicated feature writer. He is the author of more than 5,000 poems and 100 books for children and adults, ranging from the 1990 Pulitzer Prize nominee *Returning to Earth* to the popular children's book *The Father Goose Treasury of Poetry for Children*. His books have been published by Disney, Random House, Scholastic, Simon & Schuster, and others. His poems for adults have been published in *Harper's*, *The New Yorker*, *Rolling Stone*, *The Saturday Evening Post* and *The Wall Street Journal*. His poems for children appear in *Highlights for Children*, *Cricket*, *Ranger Rick*, *Humpty Dumpty*, *Jack and Jill*, *Spider*, *Ladybug*, *Babybug*, *Caterpillar*, *Children's Digest* and *The School Magazine*.

Ghigna served as poet-in-residence at the Alabama School of Fine Arts and instructor of creative writing at Samford University, and has received fellowship grants and various awards and recognitions from the John F. Kennedy Center for the Performing Arts, the Mary Roberts Rinehart Foundation, the Rockefeller Brothers Fund, the National Endowment for the Arts, and the Library of Congress. A popular speaker at schools, colleges, conferences, and libraries, Ghigna has spoken at the American Library in Paris, at schools in South America and Alaska, and at other events throughout the U.S. and overseas.

For more information, please visit **FatherGoose.com.**

Andi Martin is an adventurer who turns history into fun! Growing up in rural Alabama, she discovered that the past is like a treasure chest full of exciting stories. She now lives in Montgomery, Alabama, with her musical husband, Andy, and their two children, Amelia and Alex. Andi's journey has taken her from the Alabama Shakespeare Festival to celebrating Alabama's 200th birthday. She has worked with the Alabama Historical Commission and Alabama Tourism Department sharing the wonders of the state. She is a graduate of the University of Alabama and loves making music in her spare time.

ABOUT THE ILLUSTRATOR

Jacqueline East has been illustrating children's books across the globe for many years, including a number of stories for Charles Ghigna. She has a BA and MA in illustration. Accompanied by varying dogs, she has had studios above a chocolate factory, in a caravan by the sea and now in her home in Bristol, United Kingdom. When not illustrating she'll be found stomping the hills with her sketchbook or dancing with the local samba band!

Coins! Coins! Coins!
We push one in each slot.
Pennies! Nickels! Dimes!
How many have you got?

One penny is a cent.
Ten pennies make a dime.
Five pennies make a nickel.
It's coin collecting time!

Twenty-five cents make a quarter.
A hundred pennies, a dollar.

Collecting coins is a barrel of fun
And makes you a wealthy scholar!

Rack 'em! Sack 'em!
Stack them tall.
Flip 'em. Spin 'em.
Watch them fall!

Collecting coins
For fun and profit.
Once you start
You'll never stop it!

One side of the coin is heads.
That side is called obverse.

The other side is tails.
That side is called reverse.

Abraham Lincoln was the first
President on the penny.
Some other coins have presidents.
Do you know how many?

Look closely at your coins.
Whose faces do you see?
Washington, Jefferson, Roosevelt,
Lincoln and Kennedy.

Each coin contains a mystery
To help you learn its history.

The mintmark letter
Shows the city of its birth.
The inscription shows the date.
That helps you know what it's worth!

The obverse side
Is where the mintmark is printed.

That letter is the city
Where the coin was minted.

San Francisco is the S.
The Denver Mint, the D.

West Point is a W.
Philadelphia is the P.

The first coins came to be
In 6th Century B.C.

Coins were made of silver and gold.
Who knows what they bought?
Who knows what they sold?

George Washington
Is on the cent from 1791.
Finding one of those
Would be lots of fun!

Say these words out loud,
They're easy to remember:
Coins are called currency
And sometimes legal tender.

Copper, nickel, zinc
Are what we use today
To make the coins we spend—
And those we put away.

Quarters were made of silver
Before 1964.

So check your quarters closely
In every jar and drawer.

A rare coin collector
Is called a numismatist,
A big word for the one who finds
The coins the others missed!

Collecting coins
For fun and profit.
Once you start
You'll never stop it!